Lighting the Way in Life's Transitions and Losses

Rays of Hope

Susan Zimmerman, LMFT, ChFC

"This is a great book for anyone dealing with grief and transitions. It validated many of my emotions felt through grief of all kinds. This book was hopeful with its remarks, encouraging with its poems, and calming with its photographs.
I highly recommend it as a gift for yourself and others."

—Brenda Elsagher, CHP, humor and motivational keynote speaker, Living & Laughing

"Susan Zimmerman's breathtakingly beautiful book is a beacon of comfort and direction in difficult times. The way she explains different emotions and situations is masterful and warmly inspiring. Her thoughtful explanations will help you make sense of your emotions and sit with them more peacefully. I have shared *Rays of Hope* widely with others who've suffered the loss of loved ones, relationships, vigor, certainty, jobs, or other losses of something cherished that is no more."

—Jody Jacobson, PhD, MSBA, the Human Skills Institute

"In Susan's beautiful poems, photographs, and calming words, love is deeply felt in every page. *Rays of Hope* is one of the best therapies you can get for the grief of life's transitions and loss. Susan is in our lives for a reason."

—Chere Bork, MS RDN, author and life coach for registered dietitians

"*Rays of Hope* is a gentle guide and companion for everyone, taken as a daily vitamin to keep you company when grief swallows you whole. Each time I read these poems and the stories behind them, I feel as though I am sitting with Susan as she holds my hand and listens, reminding me it's safe to let the tears out of my body at last, there's no rush, and she'll be here when it's over."

—Roxanne Sadovsky, MA, MFA, CMHC, writer, teacher, therapist

"The uniqueness of this book is that it offers us guideposts for finding our way when life takes challenging turns, along with poetry that is calming and reflective. Susan's photographs exquisitely tie it all together."

—Gaye Lindfors, speaker and author of *This is Livin'! Learning to Move from Messy Moments to Happy Places*

"*Rays of Hope* is the perfect book to use for self-care, then to gift, and finally, to treasure. The power, wisdom, and penetrating words and photography will sear your heart and soul.

"Poetry has the power to speak of time and place, but last for years with timelessness. Few experiences and forms of art can transcend the time in which they are written. Susan's poetry has that power."

—Sharon Wegscheider-Cruse, author of *Caregiving: Hope and Health for Caregiving Families*, consultant, family therapist

RAYS OF HOPE © copyright 2021 by Susan Zimmerman, ChFC, LMFT, Mindful Asset Planning, Apple Valley, MN. All rights reserved. No part of this book may be reproduced in any form whatsoever, by photography or xerography or by any other means, by broadcast or transmission, by translation into any kind of language, nor by recording electronically or otherwise, without permission in writing from the author, except by a reviewer, who may quote brief passages in critical articles or reviews.

ISBN 13: 978-1-63489-397-8

Library of Congress Catalog Number: 2020918299
Printed in the United States of America
First Printing: 2021
25 24 23 22 21   5 4 3 2 1

Photography by Susan Zimmerman, ChFC, LMFT
Cover design by Patrick Maloney
Interior design by Cindy Samargia Laun

Wise Ink Creative Publishing
807 Broadway St. NE, Suite 46
Minneapolis, MN 55413
wiseink.com

I met Kent in a men's small group. He, like many others he helped, consulted with me on business and startups. He will be missed. May this book help you on your grief journey.

To

The family of Kent

From

Dan Heier

*May these words
and nature's beauty
help you find rays of hope
to comfort and encourage you
during challenging transitions*

This book is dedicated to
your life's loves and lessons

INTRODUCTION: RAYS OF HOPE ... 12
"A Heartening Blend" 15
A HOPE Mindset 16
When to Seek Help 19

LIFE TRANSITIONS 20
"Hope's Glow" 22
Recognition of Transitioning 23
The Meaning of GRIP 23
"Transition Condition" 24
Unique and Varied 26
"Soothing Voice" 26
"Devoted Courage" 27

STAGES OF GRIEF 28
"Good Grief!" 32
Grief Stages as NEAR 33
Early Reactions to Loss 35
"Ocean of Emotion" 36
"Off Course" 38
Anticipatory Grief and Anxiety 39
"Anticipating" 40

TRANSITIONS OF LOSS 42

Young Loss 43
   "Aching Heart" 43
Natural Order Loss... 44
   "A Young Leader" 44
Children... 46
   "Lost Future" 47
   "Disbelief" 48
Fragile Losses 50
   "Yearning" 50
Previous Generations... 52
   "Parentless" 53
Caring Consolers... 54
   "Good Mourning Friends" 55
   "Listening Gratitude" 56

OTHER LIFE TRANSITIONS 60

Broken Relationships 62
   "Starting Over" 63
Loss of Animal Companionship 64
   "Pet Passage".. 65
Change in Residence 66
   "Moving Is a Moving Experience".....................67
Empty Nest.. 68
   "Soaring Always" 69
Changes in Health.. 70
   "Bossy Aging!" 72
   "Continuing On" 75

Job Loss or Change 76
   "A New Field" 76
Lost Childhoods 78
   "Unblocking" 79
   "Inner Radiance" 81

PROCESSING YOUR FEELINGS 82

Contradictory Feelings 84
   "Empty on Full" 84
Tears and More 86
   "Not Meant to be Tame" 87
   "Release" 88
   "Nature's Tears" 90
   "Holding On" 93
Letting Go 94
   "Letting Go" 95
Infinite Layers 96
   "Endless Dimensions" 96
Mental Preparation 98
   "Passing Thoughts" 99
Made New 100
   "In Spirit" 100

TRANSFORMATIVE GROWTH 104

Forgiveness 105
   "Power to Comfort" 107
Different Responses to Grief 108
   "Unique Journeys" 109
   "Reflection" 110

Symbolic Comforts 112
"Cuff Link" 112
The Power of Private Ceremonies 114
"Peaceful Lingering" 114
Firsts 118
"First Snow" 119
"Autumn Angels" 120

CONTINUANCE 122

"A New Beginning" 123
Journaling Through Loss 124
The Healing Art of Poetry 126
"Dancing Falls" 127
Therapeutic Poetry 128
The First Poem 130
For You Now 131

CONCLUSION 132

"HOPE" 137

ABOUT 138

About the Author 139
Acknowledgments 140
Bibliography 142
Order Information 144

INTRODUCTION:
Rays of Hope

It has been an honor to create therapeutic poetry, prose, and even a few acronyms for the *Rays of Hope* books in combination with nature scenes that I've had the pleasure to photograph over many years. Many people have expressed a sense of calm from the blend of words and pictures. My hope is that you will find comfort and encouragement in their beauty and messages.

People have asked me why I specialized in grief and have written about it. Professionally, it began with an intense experience during my psychology training. I'd enrolled in a class about addiction and alcoholic family systems. The class was highly interactive, taught predominantly with demonstrations of actual therapy. As a student, I was shocked by the countless stories of traumatic and abusive childhoods and was deeply affected by the participants' sadness and grief. The only thing I was confident of was that I needed more education! I wanted to help bring hope and light to people who had suffered traumatic losses.

A few weeks later, my dad was diagnosed with terminal cancer. I still remember my mother's voice on the phone when she relayed the news. It was the day before Thanksgiving. He wasn't going to get better. In his mid-sixties, he'd worked hard his entire life and had just retired the year before. Suddenly, retirement was all about cancer.

I learned that mourning invades you whether you're ready or not, even when it's the anticipation of losing a loved one while they're still with you. You become both griever and consoler as you wrestle with your emotions while attempting to console others. Education is powerful and powerless at the same time. It helps ease the way, but it does not allow you to opt out of grief. Never before had I felt angry at someone's body. Now I was furious at Dad's body for betraying him.

Dad became deeply reflective as he seemed to be reviewing his life. He had some sorrows he'd never given voice to, and for the first time in his life, he wanted to talk about them. I felt untrusting of this new part of him. I was terrified that talking about it might cause him emotional distress that would hasten his cancer's progression and shorten his life even more. Education and therapy colleagues helped me overcome this worry and find the courage to converse with Dad about what was on his mind. This opened the door for him to share his own grief, shed his many tears, and grieve his losses. He discovered a profound peacefulness that was a gift to himself and everyone who loved him.

When education and hope light the way, we get a vital and needed glimpse of feeling better. Creative outlets can provide a powerful aid to finding additional coping methods to help us through the pain of grief. In "A Heartening Blend," we see the hint of hope's appearance as the benefit received from searching for the courage to cope with loss.

A Heartening Blend

*We wonder if there's a ray of hope,
While fearing we can't possibly cope.*

*Lost in mourning, we're unsure what to seek,
But if we keep searching, sometimes braving a peek,*

*Two miracles will appear in a heartening blend,
One we'll find in nature, the other in a friend.*

> "Sometimes our candle goes out, but is blown into flame by an encounter with another human being."
>
> —Albert Schweitzer

A HOPE Mindset

During your transition experiences, it's wise to retain a few tools that will help you remember useful guidelines for coping when new struggles emerge. Reactions to loss rarely follow a straight line; there will be times when you encounter unexpected stumbling blocks. To move through such "chunky challenges," try incorporating the acronym HOPE into your mindset:

Honor: Respect your emotions during grief and transitions. Your journey is your own.
Open: Be open to what you encounter to help you choose growth even in the unfamiliar.
Persevere: Carry on even when you struggle and feel like giving up. Ask for help.
Encourage: Be courageous as you navigate through; it will help you find new hope.

A HOPE mindset is a powerful ally as you take in the poems and messages in *Rays of Hope*. They reflect different aspects of the emotional excursion through transitions and grief. Some may provide ideas about additional ways you can move through your journey with ceremonies or symbols that honor treasured memories. The combination of poetry and prose is designed to help make the tiniest glimmers of hope appear in the transformational potential inherent in healthy mourning of a loss.

The phrase "loved one" typically refers to a special person in your life. For the purpose of understanding the elements of grief that can happen in many life transitions, it's useful to expand "loved one" to include loved aspects about your life stages, familiar surroundings or activities, or other favorite things about your life.

A poem about grieving the loss of a loved one may also give us insights into moving through other life transitions. It's helpful to consciously watch for those insights. Some poems may provide validation of feelings you have had but have not felt comfortable sharing. Keep in mind too that life transitions or losses may vary considerably, but the grief process from different circumstances can have considerable similarity. For example, the celebration of a newly emptied nest can flow into a sense of loss as a beloved child is no longer a daily presence in the home.

Poetry can be a comforting companion in your journey through transitions. Like a painting, photograph, or music, it can touch your heart in ways that ordinary words cannot. It may help you reach that place that needs to be found deep inside you. Poetry can help you cry, but it can also help you laugh again. Sometimes it brings you a sigh of relief, a relaxed moment, or some refreshing, deep breaths. A poem can encourage your movement through life's losses. A single word, rhyme, or rhythm often creates a soothing sensation or a meaningful insight. All that's required is attention and an open heart with a desire to honor your grief rather than deny it.

Loss is something we all experience in life, yet most of us, even as adults, have received precious little education about how to grieve significant losses in healthy, helpful ways. Society often pressures us to try to rush past it and attempt to avoid the natural suffering that loss and change entail. Grief, in its simplest definition, is deep sadness or emotional distress. It is a natural reaction to loss.

Our own suffering may be intensified due to myths about youth, love, success, or materialism. Enlightenment is found in our movement through grief by challenging the myth that we can ignore, control, or opt out of mourning. There is no absolute correct or incorrect way to grieve, but it's important to respect it.

Especially when a loss is sudden or unexpected, an attempted resistance to suffering leaves us poorly equipped to cope. We discover that, to some extent, we have bought into the belief that painful emotions or circumstances are optional. We mistakenly believe that we should be able to achieve our way out of it or just get busy and escape our pain, and that the faster we ignore it, the better off we will be. But when this is what's practiced, all too often our buried grief manifests in other ways, including health problems or behaviors that hurt those we love the most. Hopefully, *Rays of Hope* can help prevent such unnecessary disharmony and difficulty. It cannot eliminate the pain of grief but can help us move through it in healthy ways, while beginning to formulate new hope for the future.

I'm profoundly thankful for the many people who've shared their transition and loss stories with me through the years. Their journeys are felt deeply in my heart and have influenced my poems and writing for this book. My hope is that the messages in *Rays of Hope* make a positive difference for all who read them. We all experience periods of grief throughout our lives, so do reread the book during each of those times. It's a new and unique journey every time.

When to Seek Help

Although this book's purpose is to help people find comfort and personal insights while moving through transitions and loss, it is not a substitute for therapy. Please seek assistance from a mental health professional if you experience a persistent, depressed sense of despair or a feeling that you do not value your own life. Substituting alcohol, drugs, or other unhealthy behaviors can result if you are unable to adjust to the loss you are experiencing. Your life holds value and the world needs your unique gifts. Professional guidance can help you gain fresh perspectives and move through grief so you can find renewed hope in your life.

Life Transitions

Transition is the process of changing from one state or condition to another. It is important to recognize that even positive transitions may trigger painful cycles of grief. Life's changes disrupt us as our comfort in the familiar vanishes into the unsettling aspect of new and different circumstances.

The poetry throughout *Rays of Hope* conveys some of the emotional challenges of life transitions or the loss of a loved one. Each poem intentionally ends with a ray of hope, even if earlier it reveals some of the most painful elements of the grieving process. "Hope's Glow" reminds us of the wide range of emotions and the subtle, sometimes barely perceptible evolution of moving through transition.

Hope's Glow

Where is hope when you're in despair,
When grief engulfs you everywhere?

Hope is the light that filters down,
A dim ray at first, upon your frown.

Hope's glow then shines into your heart,
And gently whispers, "Once more, start."

It warms you from the inside out,
And in that warmth, you move through doubt.

Next thing you know, faith tiptoes in,
Beaming bright upon your long-lost grin.

Hope and faith shine together with love,
To light your path from powers above.

Recognition of Transitioning

A colleague of mine used to frequently and humorously exclaim, "I've got to get a *grip!*" His emphasis on the word *grip* made it stand out memorably. Next he'd proceed to rapidly list his most recent stressors and inability to keep up with all the disruptive changes in his life. He was expressing his recognition of needing to find a way to manage his emotional response to the challenges he was experiencing.

When I happened to find a baseball cap in a gift shop that had the phrase "Get a GRIP" boldly printed on it, I couldn't resist getting it. Given my fondness for acronyms as a teaching tool, I created one for the word GRIP. Its purpose was to serve as a reminder of how we can therapeutically process our life's changes, losses, stressors, or transitions.

The Meaning of GRIP

GRIP stands for **G**one, **R**emains, **I**s **P**ossible. The acronym's words are meant to remind us to think through or, better yet, write answers to these questions when experiencing difficult transitions:

What is **G**one?
What **R**emains?
What **I**s **P**ossible?

By identifying the source of loss, we face more clearly what is gone. Noticing the many positive elements that still remain creates the realization that not all is lost, even though it may feel like it in the moment. Identifying positive possibilities, then, creates a glimmer of relief and optimism about the future. I highly recommend this "Get a GRIP" exercise to help elevate your spirit when change is causing high stress, discouragement, or grief.

In the next poem, "Transition Condition," we see some of the natural reactions that may occur as we find ourselves in the new and unfamiliar territory of transitions in life. The ray of hope shines brilliantly when we find our courage to navigate through.

Transition Condition

Transitions in life
Impose changes we expected,
But others show up
We'd never suspected.

Health and friendships start shifting
Some are sad, some uplifting.
Homes have downsized or grown
What comes next is unknown.

It's hard to feel ready
With emotions unsteady.
Like a churning river,
We feel ourselves quiver.

And when our favorite
Grand designs crumble,
We search for someone
To whom we can grumble.

Transitions' terrain
Is cluttered and bumpy.
Moving forward with caution,
We feel a bit jumpy.

Disruptions invite us
To navigate changes.
And when we stay open,
Our path rearranges.

It shows us the direction
For finding new hope,
And lights the way
To help us peacefully cope.

Unique and Varied

People vary in their need for expression in times of transition. Everyone's process is unique. Some are more naturally verbal than others. Most need outlets to express their sorrow at one time or another, even if it is brief. There may be times when you end up sharing an aspect of your grief that you had not intended and it becomes a gift of simple validation. This can be seen in the poem "Soothing Voice." Learning to trust in our own sharing can be a valuable discovery, one for which the risk was worth taking.

Soothing Voice

I found my way to a quiet place,
intent to not speak a word.
And then came the soothing voice of Grace,
who inspired me to be heard.

The many facets of coping with loss and change require us to take heart. One definition of heart is courage. Courage does not mean the absence of fear. Courage is the determination to do something that we know is difficult.

Simple in its message, "Devoted Courage" reminds us that devotion is an important component in finding the necessary courage to work through fearful parts of our grief.

Devoted Courage

The path to courage is blazed by fear,
We can't have one unless the other's near.
With devotion, then, toward each we'll steer,
Embracing both and holding them dear.

"Courage means, literally, 'heart-ness'—having heart. Its opposite is not cowardice but heartlessness. Have heart and take heart— and you will always be courageous."

—Linus Mundy

Stages of Grief

Given that grieving can be a tremendously confusing and painful time with much uncertainty, it can feel like climbing mountains in the fog. We aren't sure what's to come, and that drains energy and creates anticipatory anxiety.

When we create and allow several channels of communication to remain open, they become the rays of hope that lighten the load, heartening us throughout the twists and turns of our transition journeys. Awareness of grief's common stages can be helpful as our human brains stubbornly attempt to anticipate and plan for a clear future.

The word *stage* is imperfect and inaccurate when describing grief, which does not progress as a single step or process. The grieving process can't be relied on to have a linear sequence nor to move in a single direction. Think of stages for this purpose, then, as commonalities of grief that have been shared in the human experience.

Elisabeth Kübler-Ross identified five stages that dying people experience:

    Shock/Denial; Anger; Depression; Bargaining; Acceptance

These stages came to also be used in discussions of grieving any loss. It is best to view them not as an assignment to complete but as a process that flows back and forth. Information about grief's motion can help us see that there is some progression to the grieving process and that the intensity of its early suffering eases over time.

Terence P. Curley, in *The Ministry of Consolers*, identifies three phases of grief:

1. Separation: Disorienting numbness, shock, avoidance, or denial
2. Transition: Multiple emotions, disorganization, transition
3. Reorganization: Readjusting to and accepting the loss

It's a relief to know you are not going crazy. That is one of the primary advantages of learning about grief stages. In *Transforming Loss*, John M. Schneider, PhD, reminds us, "We don't 'get over' a significant loss, but we can move on. Instead of getting over what we lost, we incorporate its meaning and its memory into the fabric of the rest of our lives."

C. S. Lewis, in *A Grief Observed*, said, "For in grief nothing 'stays put.' One keeps on emerging from a phase, but it always recurs. Round and round. Everything repeats. Am I going in circles or dare I hope I am on a spiral?"

In the poem "Good Grief," we see what can happen if we try to overanalyze our grief or force it to follow a prescribed pattern.

Good Grief!

Books say grief comes in stages, well sometimes I think it's true.
The first one is denial, but right now I am so blue.
Oh, that comes after anger, good grief—I can't get it right!
So, after I am mad, then sad, acceptance is in sight?

Only after I've done bargaining, a book is telling me,
That I can accept this painful loss. Good grief, must I agree?
No, I must not, but still I may, for one thing I feel sure.
No matter what stage I am in, I know I must endure.

Forget it! I don't want to, so right back to denial I go.
I can't believe my loved one's gone; I'm just sure it can't be so.
Then I wake up to another day, my thoughts have changed again.
I feel some peace, I don't know why, in simple remembering when . . .

They may come out of order, and predictable they're not.
Grief stages will move back and forth, with none that should be fought.
For as we suffer through our loss, in grief we can also find
All new dimensions of our love and connections that are kind.

The phases of grief flow back and forth and tend not to be helped when anyone tries to rush them along, stay stuck in them, or deny them entirely. It is common to feel numbness and disbelief in early stages, but that can return even in later periods, possibly triggered by an anniversary or other life events. Finding ways to stay connected to our loved ones and our own needs is important at all stages of grief.

Grief Stages as NEAR

I created the acronym **NEAR** to simplify and remember the common experiences of grief:

Numb
Emotional
Adjusting
Rebuilding

In pondering the phrase, "Grief is NEAR," it can feel overwhelming, like we're being swept away by seemingly endless waterfalls. We transition through significant changes throughout our lives and even the positive ones involve saying goodbye to someone or something. Given that reality, it can be healthy to accept that grief does enter our lives with some frequency. Mourning, like all emotions, has a range from mild to severe.

It is helpful to recognize grief when we are experiencing it and respect the emotions we feel. Here's more about the acronym **NEAR:**

Numbness is a natural reaction containing a form of denial that helps us cope in the earliest experience of grief. The shock of loss and change has a numbing effect as our minds and bodies need time to begin preparing to feel subsequent emotions.

Emotions that emerge vary considerably and can take months or years before being felt. Often the emotional journey brings feelings we have never experienced before in our lives. Their sheer breadth and prevalence are unsettling and difficult. It is important to remember that these emotions, while painful, are most often temporary. Their intensity and frequency typically diminish as we continue to move through life.

Adjusting is what we begin to do as we advance through the emotions of coping with loss and change. When we progress into phasing in adjustments, it signifies a natural shift in focus with contemplation that allows us to envision the future again. Acceptance can be an exceedingly difficult concept to feel ready for, but adjusting feels tolerable. Sometimes the process of adjusting helps us move toward acceptance. This is when we discover we have regained some feeling of capability for making decisions that integrate changes into our lives.

Rebuilding is when we take actions to reconstruct our lives after our loss. This can include significant movements, such as a change in residence, or smaller actions like rejoining a book club. As we regain clearer thinking and renewed activities, feelings of encouragement tend to return, even though there is a mix of emotions that move back and forth.

Early Reactions to Loss

In the early weeks following the loss of a loved one, painful emotions seem to dominate our being. We are forced to contend with the shocking reality of our loved one's absence in our life and the many dimensions associated with the loss. At times, even a sense of hopelessness or despair seems to be our new forever reality.

Exhaustion and apathy seem to take over our being. But it's important to know the intensity of such feelings is rarely permanent. In our fast-paced, achievement-oriented society, we may suspect we are failing or even going crazy. These are common responses, so try not to judge yourself harshly or apply societal timetables to your personal experience of grief.

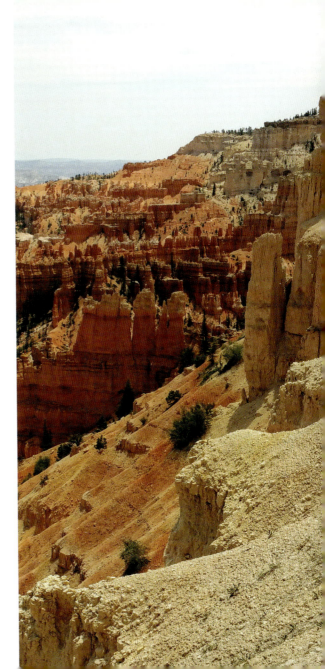

Ocean of Emotion

We rarely know the depths of our soul,
Until loss plays its hazardous role.
Emotions plunge as deep as the sea,
And into the sky we want to flee.
Then comes a day it seems we'll make it through.
Crashing waves have calmed, transforming the view.

Emotions, especially new and unfamiliar ones, can be frightening in their potency. "Ocean of Emotion" captures the depth and ferocious aspect of grief. The sheer variety, intensity, and unpredictability of such emotions can make you want to flee them. But neither flight nor fight makes them vanish and can instead cause new waves of emotion to churn back into our experience of loss, prolonging the difficulty. If we learn to accept the flow and motion of our emotion, the waves do calm, and our view eventually transforms into a more serene one.

Off Course

Some journeys must be made alone.
The path through grief we make our own.

It may be eased when a love's light is shown
To help take new steps instead of postpone.

One truth exists, off course we'll be thrown.
Our dreams have changed, though to what is unknown.

Grief's route and timing some may not condone.
We might even sense a disapproving tone.

That can't be our guide through this difficult zone;
Inner faith and courage are how we are grown.

Some describe mourning as being caught in a forceful storm that blows us about so fiercely that we cannot emerge from it unchanged. Every grief experience is unique, even if we have a shared loss with someone close to us, as conveyed in "Off Course." We may have some common experiences with others in grief, which is comforting, but it does not eliminate our suffering. Nor does it eliminate the need to honor our own way of navigating through. Usually there are some altered ways of envisioning and living life after a significant loss. Our society may appear unsympathetic in many ways, so it is up to us to make our way through these changes. Personal courage becomes our vital ally.

Anticipatory Grief and Anxiety

When we receive upsetting news about important aspects of our lives such as our health or that of a loved one, jobs, relationships, the economy, or world events, we experience a form of grief. It is natural for an unsettling feeling to develop that results from anticipating the loss of a loved one or a significant aspect of our lives. In addition, with news that reveals the possibility of worsening difficult events, it triggers a psychological response known as anticipatory anxiety.

Anticipatory grief and anxiety are often paired together, causing the uneasiness of multiple worries as we anticipate how we will cope with the impending event should it occur. It is particularly difficult emotionally, as it orbits around many uncertainties. The human brain is wired to sound alarms to prepare us for danger. As worries multiply, it takes an emotional toll given the unknowns that reside in this element of anticipated pain or loss.

In the poem, "Anticipating," we see an example of the ruminating thoughts that can churn in our minds, as in the case of anticipating loss of a loved one. It is most helpful to be aware of anticipatory thinking, so you can "remind your mind to rewind" back to the present. We may have to remind ourselves frequently to set future worries aside and deal solely with present matters.

Anticipating

The diagnosis comes as a jolting shock
I hear it ticking as I stare at the clock.
Let the time slow down; we don't want to lose you
There's still much remaining in life left to do.

You were healthy and vibrant just last month
Frisky, even, a rascal with a pounce.
Like a puppy, you went romping through the park
Teasing the children, you even let out a bark!

What is the treatment? When might we know?
Where will you be? Can't something be slow?
It just can't be time for you to go
We'll love you forever, you know.

A helpful exercise is to sit calmly with eyes closed and visualize your anticipatory worries as a bundle of tangled string that you can place into a locked container. You have the key to open the container to begin the task of untangling the worries, if and when you feel ready to do so.

Transitions of Loss

Young Loss

When a child or young person dies, grief bears an especially overwhelming sense of betrayal. The natural order of things has been thrown off, and the feeling of injustice makes grief more excruciating. As expressed in the poem "Aching Heart," the shock and loss are agonizing.

Aching Heart

I cannot grasp how it can be.
This youth is gone instead of me.
So much ahead, so much to come,
That future gone makes our hearts numb.

I knew her well, but not enough.
We'll have more time, was my mind's bluff.
She never leaves this aching heart.
Who could have known we'd have to part?

These poems soothe to help us cope.
We sense her soul and cling to hope.
There is beauty remaining too,
Lives touching lives as angels flew.

Sometimes guilty feelings invade our minds over things we didn't get done or the conversations that never happened because we believed there would be more time to do so in the future. Grieving, no matter the loss, involves forgiving ourselves, even if it would not have been possible to anticipate the loss or do everything we wished we could have done had the future not been taken from the relationship. Poetry offers one of many creative outlets that can soothe us during our grief.

Natural Order Loss

When the expected natural order of things is upset by a premature death, it can be particularly devastating to older people, who often feel they should have gone first. "A Young Leader" shares the shock and struggle of such an experience, while sharing a calming visualization. We can learn from, and be led in a spiritually uplifting way by, these young souls.

A Young Leader

None of us ever thought it would be you
Leading the way to the next life's view.
It seemed your life had just begun
And was so far from being done.

We are the elders, so unprepared
For youth gone first—a thought never dared.
We assumed we'd be the ones to lead
An order in life and death to heed.

But these are things beyond our control.
You've led the way, so we'll follow your soul.
Your life is now enfolded in ours,
And over us your spirit towers.

Children

It is impossible for words to adequately express the agony of losing a child. It has been said that when our parents die, we are grieving a large part of the past. When a child dies we grieve for the past, but even more intensely for what was yet to come, as reflected in "Lost Future."

Lost Future

We lived, in part, just to see their smiles
To lose ourselves in their needs and styles.
Their faces fill our hearts and special frames,
They'd never let us forget to play some games.

Some joys they brought whizzed right on by,
Busy days vanished, tucked in with a sigh.
If they leave this earth before we do,
We'll rely on love to help us through.

There will always be some disbelief
That we are left with aching grief.
They would not want us to stop all play,
So, with their spirit, we'll find a way.

> "Death leaves a heartache no one can heal,
> love leaves a memory no one can steal."
>
> —Irish headstone

"Disbelief" reflects the inconsolable suffering of losing a child. As an encouragement to continue the connection with caring people and the spirit of the lost child, it generates a ray of hope for the future.

Disbelief

We hold each other in our disbelief.
Will a hug, gentle words, bring some relief?

Yes, some, but not where the deepest hurt lies,
That truth is visible in both our eyes.

Yet in our reaching and touching, we feel
A soulful memory to help us heal.

Receiving validation in our grief is one of our most important needs. Whether that comes from our religion, therapy, or from a consoling friend, it can help us begin to mend. Healing is something difficult to identify and nearly impossible to measure. But the combination of caring people, special places, and ceremonies often becomes the foundation of new hope.

Fragile Losses

When an infant or pregnancy is lost, parents and family members grieve the loss of life and the abundance of dreams that would have come with the growth of a child.

"Yearning" honors those fragile losses and embraces the memory of the cherished soul that will live on in spirit.

Yearning

*Dear precious baby, I grieve for you so
I yearn to hold you and to not let go.*

*Your tiny soul created many dreams
Each one shining bright, like brilliant sunbeams.*

*There were many more than I even knew
Now they dance before me, crystal clear in view.*

*The loss of your life and these dreams we grieve
Is as big as the sun, yet hard to believe.*

*So, though we mourn, we'll never depart
For your soul will live on, deep in our heart.*

Previous Generations

When a parent or grandparent dies, the disorientation of the loss has its own manifestation of surprise, even if they'd lived a long life. We're not spared from grieving, regardless of their age, their health, their readiness to depart, or the nature of our relationship with them. At times we're despondent in our thoughts, as we realize the permanence of lost dreams that hadn't occurred and never will.

Our elders' histories are part of us, and their significance tends to grow within us as we continue through our lives.

> "For life and death are one, even as the river and the sea are one."
>
> —Kahlil Gibran

Parentless

There's never a readiness
Only blank unsteadiness
When a mother or father passes
Bewildered memory clashes

Where did her recipe go?
It seems we'll never know.
How did he fix that leak?
Why didn't we take a peek?

The void is unexpected
Can't get ourselves collected
No matter their age or ours,
We're numbed by funeral flowers.

So many questions we failed to ask
To understand their lifetime's past
What were their biggest dreams?
What made them want to scream?

No matter how many years float by
There are still times we have to cry.
Missing them in old and new ways,
Our musings evolve and always amaze.

Caring Consolers

Every loss that is part of our journey carves out a new life for us. It may produce significant change or just modify a small element of our everyday life. Some find that viewing it as a new life or a new normal can help them cope and continue.

Endings always create new beginnings, even if they were never part of our wishes or our plans. "Good Mourning Friends" shows us the pleasantness of encounters with caring people who console us, or a reconnection with our spiritual life that helps us as we mourn.

Good Mourning Friends

When our hearts are grieving, we may feel despair,
It's foreign, unwelcome, seems beyond repair.

"How can we take this suffering?" is our question that cries out,
And sometimes when we cannot move, a friend shows us the route.

A quiet chat, a heartfelt note, or a story that is shared
becomes the path that guides the way, just knowing someone cared.

For our loss has brought new hearts to us to help our spirits rise.
The kindness shared between us is a mighty pleasant surprise.

Listening Gratitude

Thank you for listening to me, friend.
Your quiet acceptance has helped me mend.

Sometimes you cry too, simply nodding your head.
You give up the words and share love pats instead.

You don't tell me to hurry, get busy, or rush,
And you've never told me to be quiet or hush.

Our tears open us up for laughter as well.
How that's helped with healing is hard to tell.

But healing is something we don't have to measure.
We're grateful for friendship that we'll always treasure.

We are often both griever and consoler, as loved ones who are mourning the same loss. One of the greatest gifts we can give and receive is to simply listen and be listened to. There are rarely perfect words to say. But some can make grief more difficult. This is not the time for criticism, jokes, or pep talks. These can be taken the wrong way and feel hurtful. Quiet listening is often the most helpful gift.

Other Life Transitions

Many of the *Rays of Hope* messages are about grieving the loss of someone who has died. With other significant losses related to life transitions, we may progress through grief cycles that share similar experiences as those due to death. Transitions involve losses that occur with changes in health, family constellation, marriage, careers, and residential moves.

Certainly, many life transitions are due to positive events, yet they still may give rise to emotions of grief because they involve the loss of familiar activities we enjoyed. This can occur with job promotions, retirement, marital changes, having a baby, adopting a child, or when children leave home to start their young adult lives. Positive transitions may be complicated at times by a mistaken belief that we have no right to feel sad because it is a celebratory event or a goal achieved. Nonetheless, change always involves some loss worth acknowledging.

Several of these transitions are explored below. It can be helpful to think of our identified losses as "loved ones" in the grieving process. A loved one, in the transition context, refers to any elements of our lives that were predictable and comfortable to us. Changes in lifestyle, status, roles, health, relationships, or even in modified habits can trigger grief cycles when our familiar routines have been uprooted.

Broken Relationships

When a significant relationship ends, it can feel as devastating as a death. It has been described as one of life's most profoundly sad, anxious, and troubling transitions. This is especially true when we did not expect the ending and, thus, were wholly unprepared. In the poem "Starting Over," shock is expressed as feeling stripped bare stemming from a sense of lost identity. To recover and move on, acknowledging mistakes and learning from them are important growth tools in many different life transitions.

Finding the courage to rebuild our life and identity as a single person brings valuable lessons that are the gift of brave honesty. As with a death, we often experience shock, numbness, anger, and regrets or remorse when a relationship ends. Even if you initiated the breakup, there is usually a surprising element of emptiness and lost identity to work through. In the transformational experience of rebuilding, we can find many positive discoveries. This is especially true when courageous honesty allows admission of errors that can be resolved to prevent similar difficulties in future relationships.

It is possible for anger to be healthy when it helps create necessary boundaries to protect us from being the target of destructive conflict. Anger can also be a positive energizing force that assists us in finding constructive solutions in our transitioning lives. In the event of extreme hostility or dangerous behaviors, therapeutic or legal intervention may be necessary so it can be managed to provide safety, prevent poor choices, and create harmony in future relationships.

When relationships end, the grief characteristics of the acronym **NEAR** (**N**umb, **E**motional, **A**djusting, **R**ebuilding) can apply and be quite useful to remember. Maintaining this awareness can help us work through the pain of a lost relationship and gain new hope.

Starting Over

We were a couple; each one was a part.
Now we are singles, each with a new start.

We feel stripped bare, our identity unknown
We're surprised at this part of being alone.

To find ourselves we look ahead and behind.
We hope we'll discover we like what we find.

We see some mistakes sprinkled with pain and regret,
But the grace we are learning we will not forget.

All lives have value even while they're adrift,
The lessons received are bravery's gift.

Loss of Animal Companionship

Just as everyone's grief is unique, so too are the relationships with animals or pets in their lives. Some pets are cherished members of the family. They may be a playmate, a service animal, a quiet companion, an entertainer, a frequent visitor to our yard, or simply a highly valued life worthy of being cared for. The absence of their companionship is keenly felt and, in most circumstances, will be grieved.

Pet Passage

*Our furry, scaled, or feathered friends
Are companions to the very end.
Our pets brought special love
Unconditional and deep
Near us when we sleep
Filling our voids with a cuddle,
A nudge, or a wiggle.
Perhaps they simply
Made us giggle.
Entertaining and sometimes funny,
We've been together like bees and honey.
When they are gone, a deep void returns,
Tumultuous emotion churns.
Our heart tumbles about and slowly learns
As it journeys through more twists and turns.
We hold our special memories dear;
Their tenderness is always near.*

Change in Residence

Throughout our lives, we may have experienced living in multiple homes and possibly in several geographic areas. Others have rarely moved, even continuing to live in their childhood homes as adults. Regardless of the frequency with which you've moved, a change in residence is no small transition. The decision to move to a different home is typically due to multiple circumstances.

Changes in health, careers, family member locations, or finances are common factors in residential choices. As with other transitions, even when it is perceived as a positive move, there are losses involved. The comfort of a familiar space is gone, and a period of unsettled or doubtful feelings is not uncommon. This sense of imbalance is seen in the poem "Moving is a Moving Experience."

Moving Is a Moving Experience

The timing is right; the decision sound.
But now there's chaos all around
Heavy stuff tumbles to the ground.
My ringing phone cannot be found
. . . Moving is a moving experience.

It's not just stuff; it's memories piled high,
Of love and laughter, of times gone by.
Stacks lean precariously, topped with a toy.
I recall him playing as a little boy
. . . Moving is a moving experience.

Towers keep mounting while I keep stacking.
My brain grows tired; my prep has been lacking.
Why am I moving? Where did the time go?
I shrug, admitting that I just don't know
. . . Moving is a moving experience.

Moved to tears again, I can't help feeling blue.
Confused, though, as I'm excited for the new,
And yet, I'm already missing the old!
Can't we just put this whole thing on hold?
. . . Moving is a moving experience.

I sigh as I pick up an old photo,
It moves me, so it gets to move with me.
I picture exactly where it will be.
Gratefully, I feel a touch of glee.
. . . Moving is a moving experience!

Empty Nest

When our primary role as parent has shifted due to children leaving home, an empty nest can trigger grief emotions. As with other changes, talking or writing about it may ease the way. In the poem "Soaring Always," we see the tug of this transition. Punctuating the grief process with rituals and celebrations can help with this as well.

"Look into nature, and then
you will understand everything better."

—Albert Einstein

Soaring Always

It has come time again to change my mind.
Empty nest looming, can't be sure what I'll find.

My baby birds will soon leave the nest to fly,
If I've helped them soar, tell me, why do I cry?

Perhaps it's never easy when a child must leave,
As parents we must find ways to celebrate and grieve.

Not all tears, we've learned, are about being sad,
Some are shed for nature's beauty and being glad;

That like the redwoods, children reach a new height,
Soaring always toward heaven while finding their light.

Changes in Health

Regardless of what is defined as old or young, most "senior citizens" express an element of surprise relative to the speed at which time has passed. Another common sentiment is that aging snuck up on them, as did the aches and pains of an older body. These commonalities are expressed in the poem "Bossy Aging" as we observe an imaginary conversation unfold with the character known as Aging. Notice a healthy hint of humor becomes a coping tool as the discussion progresses.

In "Continuing On," some of the extraordinary challenges of coping with a disabling illness or injury are expressed. A decline in health has its own grief journey in dealing with multiple losses. This includes the sense of powerlessness, the unexpected shock of such changes, the social component, and the degree of pain and hardship it brings. To manage the ongoing difficulty, inner strength is called upon to grow tremendously.

It's a new experience, adjusting to age-related or other serious illnesses, injuries, pain, and the loss of wellness or vitality of our youth. As with so many life transitions, learning to focus on the positives that remain in the present is our best ally in navigating through the challenges.

Bossy Aging!

It started with a shoulder
Refusing to reach up high.
"This is common with aging,
Give physical therapy a try."

Who knew the doctor's casual words
Would be repeated so frequently?
"It's aging" that was blamed again,
For a hip hitch, then a knee.

This person in the mirror we don't recognize.
When was it those wrinkles surrounded our eyes?
Tell me, why does everything seem to droop?
Come on, now, Aging, give me the scoop!

Forgetfulness increasing, we shrug,
Hoping the answer comes with a hug.
What was the name of that movie star?
You know, the one who played the guitar?

Hey, Aging, how clever and sneaky you are
As you quietly hide out lurking near, not far.
To slow us down, you shout, "No more of that!"
"Stop those cartwheels, stop going up to bat!"

What a bossy one you are, Aging!
Couldn't you have given us a clue
That while we lived our busy lives,
Our bodies were becoming new?

Not the kind of new we used to know
That meant shiny, alert, and speedy,
But a new that means we're slowing down
And in new respects, we're needy.

Hey, Aging, we're on to your sly, wily tricks
So, we're bracing ourselves for your special mix,
Of ailments and frailties that have no fix
And seem to hit us like a ton of bricks.

Although the vigor of our youth may be gone
We've got many systems that are still switched on.
They are worthwhile, even giving us smiles
As we press on to go our lives' extra miles!

Continuing On

When a disabling illness or injury arrives,
There are days you wonder why you survived.
It seems a lifetime ago, too long to recall,
When your body was well, and you had it all.

Unthought of, this thing that took control,
Imposing on you its powerful role.
It gets to choose the degree of pain,
The duration, the when, even the aim,

Of these days you endure in the present.
It was long ago that your body felt pleasant.
Loved ones and friends may not understand
When you want to refuse a helping hand.

But your new self is trying to get acquainted
With a body so foreign, it simply feels tainted.
It's taken away your glad, social voice;
Isolation now seems the logical choice.

You're humbled, mad, baffled, and sad.
You've never felt so scantily clad
With what you'll need for continuing on
As you learn to cope with what now is gone.

Finding great courage, tolerance, and wonder,
You make your way both over and under
The mighty forces that try to defeat you.
Your inner strength grows to cope with what's new.

Job Loss or Change

Some jobs are lost by choice, as in a planned retirement, while others may vanish abruptly due to terminations caused by economic or other changes. Whether by choice or not, our work creates roles and identities for us that give us a sense of purpose.

When employment ends, even if it was by choice and seen as a positive accomplishment of a goal, there can be a confusing adjustment period. Sorrow, anger, uncertainty, apathy, or emptiness are common. There may be a sense that we lack purpose because of discontinuing our work. As with relationship endings, we find it's vital to discover who we are in the context of the multiple changed roles and daily routines.

A New Field

I never thought I'd hear myself say,
"I miss my job almost every day."
I thought I'd love the loss of stress,
Of racing time and chasing success.

Though true for a while, it wasn't to last,
I'd forgotten to change the "me" of the past.
So, I began to rebuild my new ID.
With talent and passion, I'd hire me!

To be the best of what I always was,
This transition too makes sense because
I can contribute based on love and skill,
Regardless of pay, I have value still.

I can now see a way to tend my new field
It was me, after all, who needed to yield.
It's quite an adventure, adjusting to change,
But new purpose is found when we rearrange.

Lost Childhoods

It is a tragic reality that many people have suffered unspeakable abuses as children. A frequent result of abuse and abandonment is an inability to discern emotions. This becomes especially challenging in times of additional loss.

One of the problems with denying painful emotions, however, is it also numbs us from experiencing joyful ones. We can see the struggle unfold in "Unblocking" and "Inner Radiance" as years of mistaken impressions about emotions tumble out.

Unblocking

Don't tell me to feel feelings, that simply wouldn't do.
I was taught to rise above them, ignoring that I'm blue.

Get off this kick, now will you? I'm fine, so leave me be!
Maybe some need feelings, but it surely isn't me.

I've got my life together, I am emotion-free.
I deny unwanted feelings, strong people know that's the key.

Don't tell me I am mourning, I haven't time for that!
If I feel any pain now, I'll get stuck right where I'm at.

Good people see the bright side, doesn't that mean skip the tears?
Isn't it weak and selfish, to cry about loss or fears?

If I don't block these feelings, that might mean I must change,
But I'm not sure I'm ready for something so new and strange . . .

. . . Did you say I'd feel joy too, if I'd dare to let grief in?
Could that be what these tears are, rolling down over my grin?

Inner Radiance

Dearest Pat was always a beautiful child,
Sweet voice, heart a song, and disposition mild.
I can see her grace as she plays in the sun,
With a smile so radiant, she's the brightest one.

Some people noticed and valued her light,
But the one she needed most was as dark as night.
And try as she might to shine on his path,
All he could reflect was his own inner wrath.

Tender child, please know he had to light his own way,
Not you, nor the stars, nor the sun's brightest ray.
Precious one, you've always had so much to give,
Come out of the darkness and let yourself live.

Your light has not left you, it's beaming about,
And though it feels dim now, it will not go out.
For the strength it had once is still a warm glow,
A gift from yourself in a bright, shiny bow!

Stop hiding, keep healing, and soon you will feel,
Your light has grown brighter—it's safe to be real.
That warm glow you sought serves you now from within,
There's none, but yourself, that you've had to win.

Though the scared child you were found no comfort or rest,
You've now found good souls, who offer it with zest.
Stick with the people who've an inner glow too,
For they can reflect back your light onto you!

Processing Your Feelings

With many transitions, we may experience a gloomy sense that nothing feels right. Our first laughter may be followed by a confused feeling of guilt, that it is somehow wrong to feel anything pleasant. But we're not meant to be infinitely miserable. There's also the possibility of creating new hope, as we feel those first moments of peacefulness which provide a glimpse of more to come. It is helpful to consciously try to notice those periods of feeling better, fleeting as they may be in the early stages. These are the builders of future rays of hope.

A widower, Dale, regretted his move to an independent living facility for seniors. To help him take inventory of his situation and revisit his decision to move, he did a GRIP exercise. What is:

Gone: *My house, yard, garden, giant oak trees, neighborhood friends, and walks—I miss them.*

Remains: *I can still visit my old neighborhood. I'm healthy overall. In fact, my health has been improving now that I'm less stressed. There's a park near my apartment that I love. I still have more than enough space. My back pain remains.*

Is Possible: *Walks in the new park are great. My improved health brings energy to socialize with my new neighbors. I might meet a special somebody! Indoor hall walks in the winter. My new space is easier to keep up. I'll see more of my children and grandchildren now that I live closer. Back pain means I'll like having no more yard care!*

After Dale completed the GRIP exercise, he said he felt calm, happier, and reassured that he'd made the right decision.

Contradictory Feelings

"Empty on Full" acknowledges the concurrent feelings of emptiness and heaviness that accompany grief, while expressing the desire to flee them both.

We experience contradictory wishes when mourning what is lost, which is conveyed in the poem's request to fill the emptiness full yet keep it light.

Empty on Full

Their presence, once, was a fragrant embrace that let us touch delight.
Their absence, now, is the unwelcome guest we wish not to invite.

Get along now, void, can't you go away? It's time that you take flight!
Can't you replace this aching emptiness with something full, yet light?

Surely that would make this heaviness leave and bring back what feels right.
Time ushers in some peaceful moments now, hope puts the rest in sight.

Tears and More

Perhaps because we believe it is expected of us, we try to contain our sorrow and our natural reactions to it. We may feel it's inappropriate to let out our grief, even when we are completely alone. Physical symptoms such as tightness in our chest, body aches, and difficulty breathing may alert us, yet we persist in trying to hold our grief in. Some may fear that if they start to cry, they won't be able to stop. But crying has a physiological and natural cessation. Trust your body and soul on this.

"Not Meant to Be Tame" reveals one of many possible releases of grief. You may feel a need to cry out your loved one's name while allowing your natural tears to flow. Let yourself cry, shout, or wail. This will help relieve your body's physical tensions of grief. We must remember to give ourselves permission to stop being so tame and controlled. We need to know we are not crazy or losing our minds; we are grieving. Grief is not meant to be tame.

Not Meant to Be Tame

I had to say your name.
At first a whisper,
Then another, not so quiet.

I had to call your name.
A whisper was not enough.
With flooding tears, my cry came louder.

I had to cry your name.
Loudly, mournfully,
Alone, breathless, yet breathing.

I had to wail your name.
Rejecting my contained grief,
Releasing a sorrow not meant to be tame.

I had to wail your name.
To connect with you,
With my soul, with love, with life.

I then could whisper your name.
And breathe deeply,
To heal.

Release

Burning tears, like a scalding lava flow.
With each release there is some letting go.

But they do not harden like the jagged black rock.
Instead, they soften, allowing hearts to unlock.

Our tears warm a path to help us navigate through.
Slow motion is flowing to form what is new.

"God wants our tears," a dear friend once told me when I'd apologized for my tears of grief. She rejected my apology, which was a wonderful gift for me in that moment. I'd judged that I should be done with crying. It was years later that I read about the healing chemicals in tears of grief. They are good medicine and are evidence of strength, not weakness. People often experience serenity and physical relief when they allow their tears to flow. "Release" conveys the many benefits of tears. Trust their healing power. In "Nature's Tears," we witness the uninhibited model that nature reveals.

> "We bereaved are not alone.
> We belong to the largest company in all the world—
> the company of those who have known suffering."
>
> —Helen Keller

Nature's Tears

Sometimes the sky
Reminds us to cry
When it's raining
Pouring
Storming!
The sky is not inhibited
Its tears are allowed to fall
Freely
In complete trust of their natural
Cessation.
Nature's tears pour down
Unconcerned
That it may be inconvenient
For others.
Falling
free
is
Beautiful
Bountiful

Holding On

This loss is something I can't bear.
How can each day seem so unfair?

I want things like they used to be.
Please bring my loved one back to me.

The hole's too big, I cannot breathe.
Does it mean that I, too, should leave?

I'll go to them, I'll find a way,
I start to plan the time, the day.

Just when that's all I can conclude,
A sunset calms my anguished feud.

A loving voice shares words of strength,
There's new life here, at any length.

It happens that loss makes us grow,
And helps us see where we can go.

"Holding On" speaks the raw truth of how unbearable the shock of losing a loved one can feel, especially if it was sudden or unexpected. There are physical as well as psychological ailments in grief. Sleeplessness, aches, and extreme fatigue are common.

Many people question whether they indeed can bear to live with their loss. Some imagine escape routes from their loss or wish they could somehow join their lost loved one. Parents who have lost a child may wish they could trade places with their child to make the natural order fit how it "should be." It takes tremendous effort to continue coping, but as we see in the poem, there is hope in simple comforts that can come from soothing words, quiet closeness with someone we trust, music, or calmly connecting with nature's beauty.

Letting Go

Ceremonies can help us recognize and feel the differences between letting go and holding on. These phrases have taken on so many meanings in our everyday language that trying to grasp them in our grief process can become tremendously confusing. The poem "Letting Go" reveals the healthy movement from a lack of acceptance to the realization that holding on drains our energy.

Although holding on is a natural part of the grief experience, it may eventually give way to letting go. Letting go does not mean ceasing to care or abandoning memories of our loved one. It means we become less resistant to the change our loss has brought about. It helps us conserve our energy as we incorporate the loss into our lives.

Letting Go

Dear loved one, I am letting you go now.
Holding on had been my secretive vow.

Tight and insistent, we'd refused to part.
Conspiring like this, I'd not have to start

To accept your absence as life goes on.
This deal could continue from dusk 'til dawn.

Now I know letting go will keep you near,
For your heart lives in many, always here.

Infinite Layers

In "Endless Dimensions," we see an example of the many exhausting layers of daily occurrences, self-identities, emotions, perspectives, and plans that we miss when we experience significant change or loss. Reminders of varying new aspects of it can occur several times daily in the early stages, often catching us by surprise. Thankfully, these realizations of loss don't come all at once, for such a flood of awareness could be too overwhelming.

Endless Dimensions

The dimensions of loss feel like endless climbing
We grow weary from all the uncertain timing.
The absence of our loved one hits us with countless surprises
The many things we miss seem to come in all shapes and sizes.

The way they liked to hold a spoon, or fold a towel just so,
Were things we barely ever noticed before they had to go.
They gave us big companionship we miss in a big way
We dream about them coming back and wishing they could stay.

Their special tailored voices when talking to our pet
Gave us little pleasures we now try not to forget.
As time goes by the layers change and we find joy in new ways
We are grateful for our memories and all our special days.

It is important to remember that grief feelings do not always arise at logical or convenient times. Awareness of additional elements of our loss is sometimes triggered by unrelated events that suddenly bring a flood of emotions that surprises us. They are legitimate emotions with both highs and lows that need no apology. It is natural to cry, even years after the loss.

Mental Preparation

"Passing Thoughts" portrays the grief stages of a dying person's experience starting with the initial numbness of denial. The acronym **NEAR** indicates common passages as: **N**umb, **E**motional, **A**djusting, **R**ebuilding. When an impending death is due to a prolonged illness, it may present an opportunity for harmonious communication during that time. This becomes a gift not only for the dying person, but for loved ones who mourn before and after the death.

If this type of communication is not possible, it can be helpful to write about what you would have liked to say, and perhaps what you would have wanted to hear, had there been the opportunity. Sometimes we must grieve the lost opportunities for those conversations or the lost dreams that might have been in the future of the relationship.

Passing Thoughts

They tell me there's no cure
That simply cannot be.
I know I must endure
My family still needs me!

A treatment plan is forming
Some comfort it will bring.
Inside I still am storming
To hope I plan to cling.

I watch my family's brave side
Forgiveness happens too.
I feel a sense of deep pride
To know they'll make it through.

Joy comes in place of my strife
My soul gives me a gift.
Hope transfers to my next life
My spirit gets a lift.

Made New

Grief is a transformational experience. Every individual moves through their journey in unique ways. New meanings continue to evolve that may honor loved ones or provide new perspectives about our own transitions, as shown with the images of "In Spirit."

> "Hope is the thing with feathers that perches in the soul, and sings the tune without the words, and never stops at all."
>
> —Emily Dickinson

In Spirit

Their spirits become the bright twinkling stars,

Shining on, lighting near, and yet so far.

So their glow appears in blossomed flowers too,

With such fragrance shared, we are made brand new.

Transformative
Growth

Forgiveness

In the next poem, letting go is compared to forgiveness because of their similarities. Both require tremendous effort, but in the process new possibilities emerge and rekindle hope. The most profound, simple, and useful definition of forgiveness that I've encountered was introduced to me by the Midwest Institute for Forgiveness Training in Minneapolis, Minnesota. According to director and trainer Mary Hayes Grieco, "Forgiveness is releasing an expectation that is causing you to suffer."

This has significant usefulness in the grieving process, given there are typically multiple aspects of severe disappointment in losing a loved one. It is rare to move through grief without uncovering some contemplation of forgiveness. We may feel wronged or have discovered mistakes that leave a consideration to forgive doctors, relatives, funeral directors, or others, including ourselves or even our departed loved one. If forgiveness is thought of as releasing an expectation that is causing our own suffering, its heaviness is eased.

Power to Comfort

Letting go of a lost loved one
Is like forgiveness in a way.
It doesn't mean that we'll forget
Or that what happened is okay.

It does mean that we'll always try
To live a life that is fulfilled.
We'll not let bitter asking "Why?"
Make all our dreams vanish, stand-stilled.

We may even find brand-new dreams
Start taking shape when we let go.
A higher spirit leads, it seems,
When we allow ourselves to grow.

Fond memories help us keep going,
Their power to comfort goes far.
Healed energy now is flowing,
When forgiveness beams like a star.

Different Responses to Grief

No two individuals grieve in the same way. Even parents grieving the devastating loss of a child will experience grief differently. People's verbal or other external displays and outlook for the future vary considerably. With couples, these differences can complicate bereavement and cause feelings of isolation and conflict, making the loss even more painful to endure. It is important to recognize that having different responses to grief does not mean that one person is mourning incorrectly. Couples need to find acceptable ways to communicate openly about some of their feelings, without expectations of an identical experience on the part of their partner. Not all feelings must be shared.

Similar mistaken expectations of family members or friends can cause feelings of isolation for grieving people when they do not receive a needed response. This can happen even during positive transitions such as a job promotion. One of the challenges of mourning is the paradox of needing to rely on people for some components of our grief yet remaining self-reliant for others.

The poems "Unique Journeys" and "Reflection" speak to these matters. Others can be remarkably helpful, but we must also learn to find ways to validate and nurture our needs from within ourselves.

Unique Journeys

My body aches to share my grief with you
For now, though, that's impossible to do.
I understand why you cannot join me
In that mournful place neither wants to be.

Our sense of this loss does not overlap
We both move, alone, without any map.
Yet down the road we discover a space
For sharing, once again, a common place.

Reflection

You were the one I thought would understand
When I reached out for a comforting hand.
But the distance was too great, our worlds too far apart
We couldn't seem to find the needed place to start.

Some grief feelings aren't meant to find their way to our voice
Silent reflection, at times, is our better personal choice.
Frightened by our solitude, the gift received becomes clear
We've learned again that we can climb new mountains of our fear.

The poem "Reflection" reflects the deep frustration and disappointment felt when we've been let down during our grief journey. Rarely, however, is a trusted friend or close family member trying to be unsupportive or cause further pain. But given the unique experience people have in their bereavement, these communication challenges and disappointments will occur in the normal encounters of the process. It is a paradox, but sometimes the solo components of our grief journey can strengthen us and get us in touch with our own courage and ability to find comfort within ourselves. It can be healthy to think of these inevitable disappointments as a gift received that helps us "climb new mountains of our fear."

Especially in the early stages of loss, we may feel despair and a heightened need to have our closest friends or family members fully understand, even join us with identical feelings. Sometimes that is possible, but often it is not. No matter how close you are to someone who is grieving the same loss, your feelings will rarely be identical. Your relationship with your lost loved one was unique. You miss different aspects of what you once had, and these are not the same as any other person who is also grieving. In this regard, "Unique Journeys" conveys the lack of alignment that may exist in the early stages of loss yet shines a ray of hope on the common places that might still be found down the road.

Symbolic Comforts

Great comfort can come from creating or keeping objects that symbolize the positive memories we want to preserve of our loved one. A participant in a grief group shared the comfort of a quilt she'd made out of fabric from her son's shirts.

Planting a garden, making a collage, or creating a small photo album from favorite pictures can be therapeutic. Or simply having special keepsakes in places where you can remember your loved one may be helpful. Our meanings and reactions to symbols often evolve over time.

"Cuff Link" is an example of how a small keepsake can become a big healer when positive meaning is applied to it. Notice how it's not a reflection of the painful aspects of the loss, but rather that it preserves the joyful elements of the relationship and the time that was shared.

Cuff Link

Your cuff link sits on my windowsill
It's almost like a peacefulness pill.
Except there's nothing that I must swallow
To find relief from feeling hollow.

And all it takes is a little glance
To remind me how you used to dance.
It finds happy memories that are best,
And puts any others right to rest.

The varied meanings give me a smile
When it links me to your special style.
One little look and I can rejoice
The time we had and our healing choice.

Our hearts touched in your final hours
The cuff link has grown healing powers.
Although at first it made me sad,
Just having it now makes me glad.

"Cuff Link" is a poem I wrote after my dad died. I'd done extensive journaling using the GRIP exercise. Below is an abbreviated version as an example of the insights it can foster:

Gone: *Hearing Dad's voice, seeing his signature on cards, asking questions I'd never thought of before, seeing that special way he rested his hand on the steering wheel, experiencing more of his new reflective self.*

Remains: *Memories, gratitude for our last conversations, forgiveness, understanding, peacefulness, relief, time with Mom, ability to continue to process grief.*

Is Possible: *New lessons will come that aren't yet clear. It's all okay; joyful memories will grow, painful memories will lessen, appreciation will expand, and sorrow will shrink.*

After this exercise, I felt a new sense of where I was at in my grief journey and felt relief that I could make it through all its complicated dimensions. GRIP exercises have always brought me powerful insights and new levels of acceptance.

The Power of Private Ceremonies

Accepting the loss of a beloved person or thing isn't something that happens with ease. Rarely is it completed in one clear or singular identified moment. Acceptance is more like a patchwork of moments that eventually piece themselves together to form a quilt of adequate comfort.

One of the things we can do to help ourselves continue to create these patches of the quilt is to find our own ways to converse with, say farewell to, and honor our departed loved ones. Prayers, lighting a special candle in remembrance, tending plants, or creating a ceremony can all be powerful tools of healing.

Peaceful Lingering

I brought some flowers to the beach
To say good-bye, for the sea I reach.

The petals bouncing in a wave
Are a happier vision than your grave.

We even chuckled, you and I,
For on wet rocks I'm not so spry.

I slipped and stumbled and thought I'd fall,
But nothing could stop this special call.

One petal left kept floating back,
As if to keep our special pact.

Your spirit lingered there a bit,
And told me I am not to quit.

That petal too then washed away,
And swept peace through another day.

The poem "Peaceful Lingering" shares visions of an ocean ceremony. In a private ritual we can create more pleasant imagery than that which may have existed at a funeral or other formal functions. Rituals can leave us with a powerful impression that our loved ones have peacefully moved on in their afterlife. Making the decision to have your own private ceremony can provide deep healing. Your relationship with your loved one was unique. It stands to reason that your own personalized observance would offer comfort that only you can uniquely feel.

There is surprising value in speaking words out loud to nature, your absent loved one, your higher power, or no one in particular. The objective is to communicate your sense of loss. Your words do not have to be perfectly planned or articulated. You may feel a strong spiritual presence that you'd not expected. Words, images, or sensations may come to you that create a peacefulness you could not have anticipated. Some people sense they have received messages that give them courage and guidance for their future. These can all be profoundly comforting.

*"That petal too then washed away,
and swept peace through another day."*

Firsts

There are many firsts that will occur after the loss of a loved one. These may be special dates such as birthdays and anniversaries. Others are events, holidays, or seasonal changes, as in the poems "First Snow" and "Autumn Angel."

Acknowledgment of a transition anniversary date, whether expressed silently or to a friend, may bring much-needed serenity. Depending on the significance of the event, a shared ceremony or ritual can provide increased comfort.

First Snow

The snow has fallen while we sleep
When we awake, we sigh and weep.

Our numb limbs feel heavy, like the new-fallen snow
Weighed down by our grief, our energy is low.

For the first snow is beauty she always cherished,
We gaze at its sparkles whispering, "You are missed."

As we stare at the branches covered in white,
Her spirit touches us to say she's all right.

A lightness sweeps in and lifts our heaviness away
We arise to move about, seeing beauty in gray.

Autumn Angels

The colors are alive and vibrant on this lovely autumn day,
I wonder what our lost ones are doing and why they couldn't stay.

Do they see the same bright colors with their many varied hues?
Or from heaven are they better, blessed with angels' special views?

I imagine that I see them flying slowly through the leaves,
Brushing in more radiant color while in and out they weave.

I don't suppose I'll ever know until my day comes too.
Until then, I'll try to see some good that's in the new.

Continuance

A New Beginning

A new beginning came from following my heart,
What a frightening place for new journeys to start!
I'd become so skilled at following orders,
I'd lost my true self, confined in others' borders.

But an insistent voice kept knocking down my walls,
It wouldn't allow me to continue my stalls.
It took every excuse and said, "That can't stop you!"
And it pumped in new courage that was long overdue.

It got me moving, taking steps I'd never dared,
And to my amazement, I kept going while scared.
Transitions bring challenges worth laboring through,
For they can give birth to an awesome new you!

Journaling Through Loss

One of the most helpful and comprehensive books about grief I recommend is called *Finding My Way: Healing and Transformation Through Loss and Grief* by John Schneider, PhD. In it, the author suggests three primary questions as a guide for discovery of our own journaling and grief awareness process:

What is lost?
What is left?
What is possible?

Although these questions are short and simple, moving through their many dimensions is neither. Courage and commitment are needed to work through our responses, but writing them down can offer tremendous insight into our own experiences. Journal entries will change as we continue moving through our grief, as our perspectives continue to evolve. It can help us restore our sense of balance and organize the complexity that engulfs us while we mourn. In writing about what is possible, we can discover positive aspects of life again.

> "When we discover within ourselves the essence of our love after losing its external form, life has cause for celebration."
>
> —John M. Schneider, PhD

The Healing Art of Poetry

In his book *Poetic Medicine*, John Fox encourages reading and writing poems, saying, "Reading poems you enjoy may plant seeds for your own writing when the time is ripe."

I encourage you to read the poem "Dancing Falls" as an invitation to write, or continue writing, your own poems. Remember, poems don't have to rhyme or have a perfect rhythm. As the writer, allow your words to flow in whatever way feels most soothing, truthful, or comforting. Like the dancing water in the falls, dancing words can create a therapeutic surprise. In that spirit, any writing can provide insights you hadn't expected.

Dancing Falls

When you get stuck it helps to rhyme,
And take a little trip through time.

Remembering love, a special touch,
Of someone you have missed so much.

Just grab your mood and write it down,
And let the rhyme make you a clown.

Or see if it can help you out
When you are sad or full of doubt.

Sometimes it even moves your soul,
And lifts you out of a dark hole.

Rhythm falls in a steady beat,
It's always fun to keep it neat.

It's also good to mess it up,
And frolic words like a young pup.

As long as you find that surprise
Of dancing words before your eyes.

Therapeutic Poetry

You have probably heard of aromatherapy. Let's give "a-*rhyme*-a-therapy" a try! This is my word to describe the therapeutic benefits of writing poetry. Poems can provide sustenance and help us keep moving during difficult times.

Every poem begins with one line, or even just one word. When we experience strong feelings and raw emotions, poetry gives us creative permission to cry out from the depth of our being.

If you feel uncertain about how to begin your poem (or journal entry), you can start with a sentence stem:

I miss . . .
I remember when . . .
How can it be that . . .

Complete the thought and then keep adding what comes to you. You may discover great delight in the nourishing surprise of finding words that rhyme and perfectly fit a feeling that otherwise seemed to have no words (or took too many words to even attempt to convey).

Maintaining a certain rhythm provides structure that, at times, creates a perspective that heightens clarity. Sometimes, in obedience to a certain rhythmic pattern, we may happen upon bits of our unconscious wisdom. We may surprise ourselves by saying something we hadn't intended at all, yet it becomes a powerful ally in our own healing. Of course, the nice thing about poetry is it doesn't have to rhyme or even keep a steady beat. It can free flow. It's all about personal preference.

Let's use one of the sample sentence stems to provide an example of both:

I miss the way we used to share a meal.
Now, without you, I'm not sure I can heal.
I remember how we'd have a quiet talk,
And after dinner we would go for a walk.

Or

I miss our meals together
Sitting quietly,
Talking about our day.
Taking walks, sharing everything.

In the samples above, similar thoughts are expressed in different forms. Writing helps uncover what is lost and can lead to discovering what is left and what is possible. Or use the prompts offered by the acronym **GRIP** (What is **G**one, **R**emains, **I**s **P**ossible), suggested earlier in the book section titled "Life Transitions." These writing exercises help you identify and cope with many elements of your transition. Studies show that simply acknowledging our stress in written form lightens it to some extent. Be sure to continue your responses in all three sections of the exercise, as this is where you'll discover the emergence of new hopes.

> "Poetry is when an emotion has found its thought and the thought has found words."
>
> —Robert Frost

The First Poem

My first poem was written for a third-grade school assignment. It was about my pet snapping turtle whom I'd found lumbering across a street in my neighborhood. I kept him for just a few days, long enough to name him Yurtle, consider him my pet, and discover his fondness for bologna. My sisters and I loved watching him snap bites out of a fresh slice of the tidy pink meat. His neck would stretch out slowly from beneath his heavy shell, and in a quick snap of a bite, a perfect triangular piece of bologna would be gone. Yurtle was fun and entertaining. Our seemingly endless supply of bologna could keep this relationship going for a long time.

One day, however, my older sister and I decided Yurtle should be set free to roam again the excitement of our neighborhood lawns and ponds. The very next morning as we crossed the street to go to school, we saw Yurtle. He hadn't stayed in the safety of our grassy yards, as we'd envisioned. Instead, it appeared, he'd headed straight for the street and hadn't survived the crossing. I felt immediately shocked and saddened at what had happened, then guilty for my part in the apparent bad decision to simply set him free. What had happened to Yurtle was gruesome and it seemed tragically unfair. Shortly after that I discovered the therapeutic value of poetry, thanks to the writing assignment. The last lines are all I remember now, but I do recall feeling some comfort in reading it multiple times:

> *Yurtle the turtle lived in a window well,*
> *Yurtle the turtle was swell.*

It was a poem about grieving and accepting a loss. I didn't know it at the time, but my own feelings of shock and sorrow had no place to go. A dead turtle—especially a squashed, roadkill one—just wasn't something anyone cared to hear about. I remained silent. No big deal, right? But Yurtle had been my pet, my responsibility for a short time, and I felt his death was my fault. The poem helped me move through this relatively minor grief and validate the loss, despite its insignificance to others in the world. Just noting the past tense word in the line, "Yurtle the turtle *was* swell," helped me accept the reality of his death. It also validated the insight that regardless of Yurtle's importance to anyone else in the universe, he had mattered to me. And that did matter. Sometimes, you must grieve alone.

The opportunity to write a poem for a school assignment provided several benefits. I was able to acknowledge my regrets, accept the loss, grieve it further, gain some new perspective, and begin to feel better. A poem can help you see and feel something that ordinary words cannot.

For You Now

Read and reread any writing that you discover helps you feel comforted or encouraged. As with repeated viewing of a favorite movie, you may be amazed at the new things you notice with each additional reading of a poem or a message that touched your heart.

Do take some moments to experiment in your journaling with all kinds of writing. Explore how the different forms make you feel. It provides a place for both painful and joyful feelings to be held. This can light the way to a clearer vision of where you've been, where you are, and where you want to go. Your writing may come in waves that help you discover your style for integrating fragmented parts of your life. Your writing is for you.

Conclusion

Throughout our transition-filled lives, we accumulate losses of many kinds. Grief has been described by the Center for Grief, Loss, and Transition in Saint Paul, Minnesota, as "a natural internal response to a significant loss that is experienced physically, emotionally, mentally, and spiritually." It impacts our entire being and is a complex human experience.

If we were not able or allowed to grieve past losses, whether they resulted from life transitions, traumatic experiences, or the death of a loved one, our unconscious minds are likely to take elements of them into each new loss. It is possible that whatever loss you are currently experiencing, you might be grieving ones from long ago as well. Cumulative grief from multiple losses that may have been unaddressed presents a compounding effect that deserves attention.

Perhaps it's time to acknowledge previously unrecognized grief of the past. Ask yourself, "Are there other losses from earlier in my life that I wasn't able to mourn?" Write your responses to see what you discover. Your journaling can lead you to the kind of attention needed for complicated or cumulative grief.

Allow yourself to be creative as you move toward transformation during your times of loss. Incorporate **HOPE** into your life transitions to help you: **H**onor your grief; remain **O**pen to what it teaches you; find ways to **P**ersevere even when you feel like giving up; and **E**ncourage yourself toward embracing your inner bravery. Like Pat in the poem "Inner Radiance," you're likely to encounter resources, people, and encouragement that help light the way, especially in times of darkness.

> *Your light has not left you; it's beaming about,*
> *And though it feels dim now, it will not go out.*
> *For the strength it had once is still a warm glow,*
> *A gift from yourself in a bright, shiny bow!*

May you continue to discover new *Rays of Hope* that light the way in your personal navigation through transition and loss. Let them shine brightly for you!

HOPE

It was once a wish, a love, or an aim.
Holding tight didn't assure a forever claim
To familiar comforts, with nothing changed,
Of never having to be rearranged.

Amidst the turmoil, along came new hope.
Slowly nudging us up the steep slope
Of coping with loss and changed conditions,
Lighting the way for our new life's transitions.

About

About the Author

Susan Zimmerman, LMFT, ChFC, is a licensed marriage and family therapist and Chartered Financial Consultant who has been helping people navigate life transitions for more than thirty years. In her psychology studies, she specialized in grief, loss, and trauma. She earned the Certified Clinical Trauma Professional (CCTP) designation in 2011 from the International Association of Trauma Professionals.

Susan is an author of several books that cover many topics including therapeutic communication, personal growth, financial psychology, and relationships. Susan has been featured in several publications, including the *Wall Street Journal*, *Washington Post*, *LA Times*, *Forbes*, *Money Magazine*, the *Chicago Tribune*, the *St. Paul Pioneer Press*, and *Psychology Today*.

Acknowledgments

To my precious family for their ongoing love and encouragement, thank you. I love you!

To our parents, who've passed on, but whose powerful lessons continue to emerge as we carry on in life. We are eternally grateful.

To Jack Canfield, coauthor of the #1 *New York Times*–bestselling Chicken Soup for the Soul® series and *The Success Principles*™, for being an enthusiastic advanced reader of *Rays of Hope* and offering priceless coaching, encouraging words, and invaluable ideas. Our discussions will be remembered and highly valued always.

To Steve and Laura Harrison, and to Patty Aubery, for their indispensable book instructions and suggestions. It made a world of difference just in time for publication!

To my colleagues, seminar participants, friends, family, and clients who entrusted their transition journeys with me, thank you. I deeply appreciate all who provided feedback about the book's contents, poems, narrative, photography, and acronyms.

To my writers group, instructed by Roxanne Sadovsky, thank you for your support and amazingly helpful feedback.

To all the readers who've sent notes expressing how the *Rays of Hope* materials have been helpful to them, thank you.

Every single story shared has been my teacher and has helped me believe in the timeless therapeutic value in *Rays of Hope*.

Bibliography

Brown, Brene. *Rising Strong: How the Ability to Reset Transforms the Way We Live, Love, Parent, and Lead.* Penguin Random House LLC, New York, NY, 2017

Cherry, Frank, and James, John W. *The Grief Recovery Handbook.* Harper & Row Publishers, Inc., New York, NY, 1988

Curley, Terence P. *The Ministry of Consolers.* The Liturgical Press, Collegeville, MN, 2004

Fisher, Bruce. *Rebuilding: When Your Relationship Ends.* Impact Publishers, San Luis Obispo, CA, 1981

Fox, John. *Poetic Medicine: The Healing Art of Poem-Making.* Penguin Putnam Inc., New York, NY, 1997

Fralich, Terry. *Cultivating Lasting Happiness: A 7-Step Guide to Mindfulness.* Pesi, LLC, Eau Claire, WI, 2007

Grieco, Mary Hayes. *Unconditional Forgiveness: A Simple and Proven Method to Forgive Everyone and Everything.* Atria Paperback, a division of Simon & Schuster, Inc., New York, NY, 2011

Hanson, Rick. *Hardwiring Happiness: The New Brain Science of Contentment, Calm, and Confidence.* Harmony Books, a division of Penguin Random House LLC, New York, NY, 2013

Jeffers, Susan. *Feel the Fear and Do It Anyway.* Ballantine Books, a division of Random House, Inc., New York, NY, 1997

Simler, Kevin, and Hanson, Robin. *The Elephant in the Brain: Hidden Motives in Everyday Life.* Oxford University Press, New York, NY, 2018

Lewis, C. S. *A Grief Observed.* HarperCollins Publishers, New York, NY, 1961, 1996

Schneider, John M. *Finding My Way: Healing and Transformation Through Loss and Grief.* Seasons Press, Colfax, WI, 1994

Schneider, John M. *Transforming Loss: A Discovery Process.* Integra Press, East Lansing, MI, 2004

Zimmerman, Susan. *Mindful Money Matters: 8 Ways to Honor Yourself and Your Financial Plan.* Mindful Asset Publishing, St. Paul, MN, 2018

Zimmerman, Susan. *Rays of Hope in Times of Loss: Courage and Comfort for Grieving Hearts.* Expert Publishing, Inc., Andover, MN, 2005

Order Information

Rays of Hope is available on Amazon.com. Give the gift of courage, comfort, and hope to help people through their transitions and grief.

For additional articles and stories about transitions and loss, visit Susan Zimmerman's blog: **www.raysofhope.us**.

Mindful Asset Planning
14530 Pennock Avenue
Apple Valley, MN 55124

Phone: 952-432-4666